I Can Clean My Room

Written by Chemise Taylor

Illustrated by Alexis B. Taylor

Copyright © 2019 by Autism Learners, LLC

Published by Autism Learners, LLC

All rights reserved. No part of this publication may be reproduced, distributed, or transmitted in any form or by any means, including photocopying, recording, or other electronic or mechanical methods, without the prior written permission of the publisher, except in the case of brief quotations embodied in critical reviews and certain other noncommercial uses permitted by copyright law.

First Printing, 2019.

ISBN: 978-1-951573-11-9

www.autismlearners.com

Playing with my toys is so much fun!
I can sit and play all day.

My dad comes in and says, "I thought I asked you to put your toys away."

...but we have to leave soon and this needs to be done."

I say, "Sure dad, no problem at all."

I start by putting
away my spotted ball.

I find more toys to put away like my blocks, sword and bear.

I find my yellow toy car. I almost forgot it was there.

I put my toys in my big brown toy chest.

This is a great way to get rid of the clutter and mess.

I close the lid.
Finally, I am all done!

I say, "Hey dad! I cleaned my room."
He says, "Good job, son!"

Book Details

Story Word Count: 138

Key Words: Clean, Up, Toys, Dad, Put, Away, Play, Done

Comprehension Check
- What was the story about?
- What did he put away?
- Who did he speak to in the story?

Reading Award

This certificate goes to:

_____

for reading "I Can Clean My Room"

Good Job!

Printable & Digital Worksheets | Flashcards | Books | Apps | More

www.autismlearners.com

www.ingramcontent.com/pod-product-compliance
Lightning Source LLC
Chambersburg PA
CBHW042111090526

44592CB00004B/81